Rockschool®

Acoustic Guitar
Grade 1

*Performance pieces, technical exercises, supporting tests and in-depth
guidance for Rockschool examinations*

All accompanying and supporting audio can be downloaded from: *www.rslawards.com/downloads*

Input the following code when prompted: **21ZNCDK1TO**

For more information, turn to page 5

www.rslawards.com

Acknowledgements

Published by Rockschool Ltd. © 2016
Catalogue Number RSK200021
ISBN: 978-1-910975-28-2
3 May 2016 | Errata details can be found at *www.rslawards.com*

SYLLABUS
Syllabus written and devised by Nik Preston and Andy G Jones
Syllabus consultants: Carl Orr and James Betteridge
Arrangements by Andy G Jones, Carl Orr and James Betteridge
Supporting Tests written by Nik Preston and Andy G Jones
Syllabus advisors: Simon Troup and Jamie Humphries

PUBLISHING
Fact Files written by Diego Kovadloff
Music engraving and book layout by Simon Troup and Jennie Troup of Digital Music Art
Proof reading and copy editing by Diego Kovadloff, Carl Orr, Mary Keene and Emily Nash
Cover design by Philip Millard
Cover photograph © Tim Mosenfelder/WireImage/Getty Images

AUDIO
Produced by Nik Preston, Andy G Jones, Carl Orr and James Betteridge
Engineered by Andy G Jones, Carl Orr, James Betteridge, Jonas Persson and Music Sales
Mixed by Ash Preston, Andy G Jones, Carl Orr and James Betteridge
Mastered by Ash Preston and Paul Richardson
Supporting Tests recorded by Andy G Jones
Executive producers: John Simpson and Norton York

MUSICIANS
Andy G Jones, Carl Orr, James Betteridge, Nik Preston, Ian Thomas, Mike Finnigan, Noel McCalla,
Patti Revell, Hannah Vasanth and Jon Tatum

SPONSORSHIP
Andy G Jones endorses Thomastik Infeld strings, Providence cables and pedal switching systems, Free The Tone effects,
JJ Guitars, Ergoplay guitar supports and Wampler Pedals. All nylon strings parts recorded direct with the Yamaha NTX2000.
Carl Orr endorses MI Audio Revelation amps & effects, and Picato strings.
James Betteridge plays Martin guitars and D'addario strings.

DISTRIBUTION
Exclusive Distributors: Music Sales Ltd

CONTACTING ROCKSCHOOL
www.rslawards.com
Telephone: +44 (0)345 460 4747
Email: *info@rslawards.com*

Awarding the
Contemporary Arts

Table of Contents

Introductions & Information

Rockschool Grade Pieces

Technical Exercises

Supporting Tests

Additional Information

Welcome to Rockschool Acoustic Guitar Grade 1

Welcome to **Rockschool's 2016 Acoustic Guitar syllabus**. This syllabus has been designed to equip all aspiring guitarists with a range of stylistically appropriate, industry relevant skills and a thoroughly engaging learning experience.

Utilising an array of well known repertoire and a truly crucial range of supporting tests, the continued progression of any student is assured from Debut through to Grade 8.

The syllabus has been authored to ensure that each student can develop as accompanists, soloists, sight readers and improvisers, whilst enabling both teacher and student to choose the areas that they wish to specialise in.

Rockschool's long standing commitment to raising academic standards, assessing industry-relevant skills and ensuring student engagement is world renowned. The 2016 Acoustic Guitar syllabus has been conceived in order to build upon this success and continue the evolution of the contemporary music world's first awarding body.

When combined with **Rockschool's 2015 Popular Music Theory syllabus**, this syllabus is guaranteed to furnish every candidate with both the practical skills and theoretical understanding necessary to perform at the highest level, across a whole range of contemporary repertoire.

Nik Preston – Head of Product Development and Publishing

Acoustic Guitar Exams
At each grade you have the option of taking one of two different types of examination:

- **Grade Exam**
  (Debut to Grade 5)
  A Grade Exam is a mixture of music performances, technical work and tests. You are required to prepare three pieces (two of which may be Free Choice Pieces) and the contents of the Technical Exercise section. This accounts for 75% of the exam marks. The other 25% consists of: either a Sight Reading or an Improvisation & Interpretation test (10%), two Ear Tests (10%), and finally you will be asked five General Musicianship Questions (5%). The pass mark is 60%.

  (Grades 6–8)
  A Grade Exam is a mixture of music performances, technical work and tests. You are required to prepare three pieces (two of which may be Free Choice Pieces) and the contents of the Technical Exercise section. This accounts for 75% of the exam marks. The other 25% consists of: a Quick Study Piece (10%), two Ear Tests (10%), and finally you will be asked five General Musicianship Questions (5%). The pass mark is 60%.

- **Performance Certificate**
  A Performance Certificate is equivalent to a Grade Exam, but in a Performance Certificate you are required to perform five pieces. A maximum of three of these can be Free Choice Pieces. Each song is marked out of 20 and the pass mark is 60%.

Book Contents
The book is divided into a number of sections:

- **Exam Pieces**
  Each exam piece is preceded by a Fact File detailing information about the original recording, the composer and the artist/s who performed it. There is also a Technical Guidance section at the end of each piece which provides insight from the arrangers as to the harmonic, melodic, rhythmic and technical nuance of each piece.

  Every exam piece is notated for acoustic guitar, but certain pieces feature two 'assessed' parts, meaning the candidate has the choice of which part they wish to perform in the exam. Certain pieces contain 'non-assessed' guitar parts, which are intended for duet/ensemble practice and performance. Likewise, certain pieces include notated vocal melodies in addition to the assessed guitar part. These have been included as reference material and to provide opportunity for duet and ensemble practice and performance. In your exam you must perform your pieces to the backing tracks provided.

- **Technical Exercises**
  There are either three or four types of technical exercise, depending on the grade:
  Group A – scales
  Group B – arpeggios/broken chords
  Group C – chord voicings
  Group D – a choice of stylistic studies. Please note, Group D only exists at Grades 6–8.

- **Supporting Tests**
  You are required to undertake three kinds of unprepared, supporting test:

  1. Sight Reading or an Improvisation & Interpretation test at Debut to Grade 5.
     Please note, these are replaced by mandatory Quick Study Pieces (QSPs) at Grades 6–8.

  2. Ear Tests: Debut to Grade 3 feature Melodic Recall and Chord Recognition.
     Grades 4–8 feature Melodic Recall and Harmonic Recall.

  3. General Musicianship Questions (GMQs), which you will be asked by the examiner at the end of each exam.
     Each book features examples of the types of unprepared tests likely to appear in the exam.
     The examiner will give you a different version in the exam.

- **General Information**
  You will find information on exam procedures, including online examination entry, marking schemes, information on Free Choice Pieces and improvisation requirements for each grade.

Audio

In addition to the Grade book, we have also provided audio in the form of backing tracks (minus assessed guitar part) and examples (including assessed guitar part) for both the pieces and the supporting tests where applicable. This can be downloaded from RSL directly at *www.rslawards.com/downloads*

You will need to input this code when prompted: **21ZNCDK1TO**

The audio files are supplied in MP3 format. Once downloaded you will be able to play them on any compatible device.

You can find further details about Rockschool's Acoustic Guitar syllabus by downloading the syllabus guide from our website: *www.rslawards.com*

All candidates should download and read the accompanying syllabus guide when using this grade book.

Acoustic Guitar Notation Explained

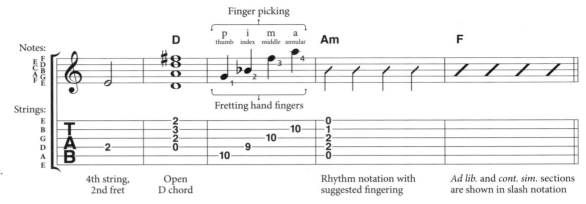

THE MUSICAL STAVE shows pitches and rhythms and is divided by lines into bars. Pitches are named after the first seven letters of the alphabet.

TABLATURE graphically represents the guitar fingerboard. Each horizontal line represents a string, and each number represents a fret.

4th string, 2nd fret   Open D chord   Rhythm notation with suggested fingering   *Ad lib.* and *cont. sim.* sections are shown in slash notation

Definitions For Special Guitar Notation

HAMMER ON: Pick the lower note, then sound the higher note by fretting it without picking.

PULL OFF: Pick the higher note then sound the lower note by lifting the finger without picking.

SLIDE: Pick the first note, then slide to the next with the same finger.

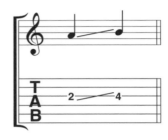

STRING BENDS: Pick the first note then bend (or release the bend) to the pitch indicated in brackets.

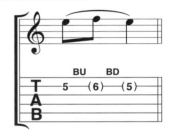

GLISSANDO: A small slide off of a note toward the end of its rhythmic duration. Do not slide 'into' the following note – subsequent notes should be repicked.

VIBRATO: Vibrate the note by bending and releasing the string smoothly and continuously.

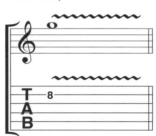

NATURAL HARMONICS: Lightly touch the string above the indicated fret then pick to sound a harmonic.

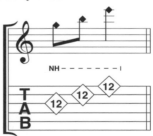

ARTIFICIAL HARMONICS: Fret the note indicated in the TAB, then (with picking hand) lightly touch the string above fret indicated between staves, and pick to sound the harmonic.

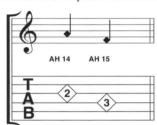

PRE-BENDS: Before picking the note, bend the string from the fret indicated between the staves, to the equivalent pitch indicated in brackets in the TAB

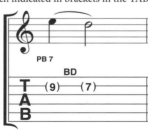

PICK HAND TAP: Strike the indicated note with a finger from the picking hand. Usually followed by a pull off.

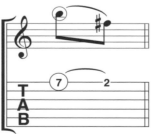

FRET HAND TAP: As pick hand tap, but use fretting hand. Usually followed by a pull off or hammer on.

QUARTER TONE BEND: Pick the note indicated and bend the string up by a quarter tone.

TRILL: Rapidly alternate between the two bracketed notes by hammering on and pulling off.

D.%. al Coda

- Go back to the sign (%), then play until the bar marked ***To Coda*** ⊕ then skip to the section marked ⊕ ***Coda***.

D.C. al Fine

- Go back to the beginning of the song and play until the bar marked ***Fine*** (end).

- Repeat bars between signs.

- When a repeated section has different endings, play the first ending only the first time and the second ending only the second time.

Metallica | The Unforgiven

SONG TITLE: THE UNFORGIVEN

ALBUM: METALLICA

LABEL: ELEKTRA

GENRE: HEAVY METAL

WRITTEN BY: JAMES HETFIELD,

KIRK HAMMET AND

LARS ULRICH

GUITAR: JAMES HETFIELD AND

KIRK HAMMET

PRODUCER: BOB ROCK,

JAMES HETFIELD AND

LARS ULRICH

UK PEAK CHART: 15

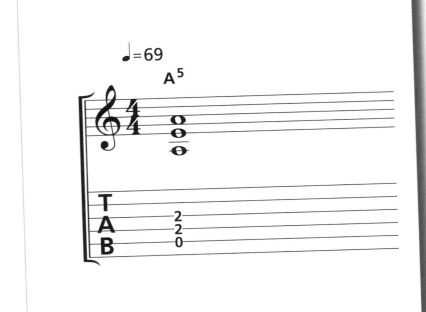

'The Unforgiven' is featured in Metallica's fifth album, *Metallica*, also known as *The Black Album*, released in 1991. The song is a power ballad. Its lyrics are about the struggle of an individual trying to fight the efforts of those who want to subjugate him. The song has been followed by two other versions dealing with the same theme but different musical content. The horn intro is played in reverse and it is taken from the classic western The Unforgiven.

The Black Album is regarded as a classic in the metal genre and it cemented Metallica's reputation, and launched the band into a stadium career. 'The Unforgiven' was covered by Vernon Reid, Frankie Banali and Tony Franklin.

Metallica are, arguably, heavy metal's biggest band. Their brand of thrash metal and heavy rock is highly acclaimed and hugely popular the world over. The band formed in 1981 and has released nine albums to date. Metallica was inducted into the Rock and Roll Hall of Fame in 2009. Their early releases contained many fast tempos and long instrumental passages underpinned by a precise delivery of complex rhythms and syncopation. This approach, as well as their lyrical approach, was changed when producer Bob Rock started working with the band in 1990. Their songs and lyrics became more streamlined and available to a wider audience as a result. Metallica also

started to explore influences other than metal in their compositions. Their sound remained powerful and direct and their live shows became hugely popular. Metallica are a stadium phenomenon worldwide. They have received nine Grammy awards to date.

The Unforgiven

Metallica

Arranged by Carl Orr

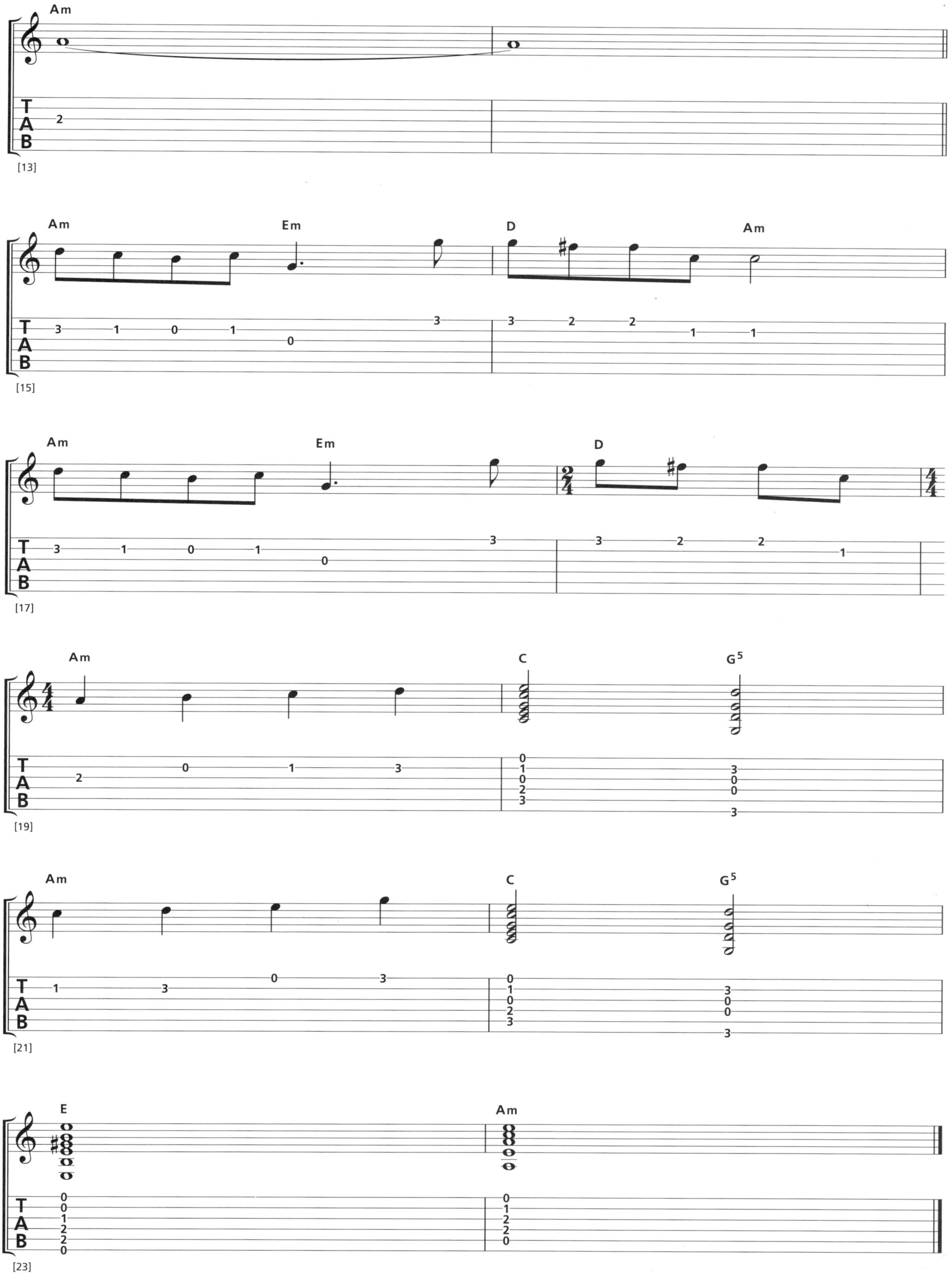
Am
[13]
Am
Em
D
Am
[15]
Am
Em
D
[17]
Am
C
G5
[19]
Am
C
G5
[21]
E
Am
[23]

The Unforgiven | Technical Guidance

This darkly atmospheric song from Metallica starts out with a mournful A5 power chord followed by a short melody, firmly establishing A minor as the key centre.

From bar 9 there are three chords from the A Natural minor scale; C major (III/mediant), G major (♭VII/subtonic) and E minor (V/dominant). On the repeat, the E minor chord is replaced with an E major chord (bar 12), giving a rich flavour of A Harmonic minor.

From bar 15 the song moves into A Dorian (minor scale with a major 6th), with the melody based on the chords A minor (tonic), E minor (V/dominant), D (IV/subdominant), moving back to A minor. The Dorian mode has quite a bright sound for a minor mode, particularly noticeable on the D chord. Two big chords follow on bar 20 and 22, C major (III) and G major (♭VII), still in the Dorian mode, and then finally that rich, colourful E (V) chord returns, leading back to the tonic on bar 24.

On the original version the melody is played by a clean-toned electric guitar, but it is easily adaptable to acoustic. The melody should be played clearly and boldly as it is the focal point of the song at this point. There are some tricky semi quavers in bars 5, 7 and 12. These can be played with alternating down and up strokes, starting on a down stroke at the beginning of each beat. The rhythm of the melody is quite subtle in places, for example in bars 5, 9, 10, 11 and 12. In these cases it is advisable to clap the rhythm first, and to apply the pitches later. In this way, the rhythmic component of the melody gets thoroughly strengthened. The rhythmic aspect is usually the weakest part in performance at this level. It is important to have a solid reference, so using a metronome is recommended. It will create a clear context for the rhythm. Without solid time, melodies that feature subtle rhythms, such as this one, tend to sound vague and abstract. From bar 15 the mood gets heavier, with the guitar stating the ominous melody in unison with the singer. The song finishes with big, bold chords.

SONG TITLE: BEAUTIFUL

ALBUM: STRIPPED

LABEL: RCA

GENRE: POP

WRITTEN BY: LINDA PERRY

PRODUCER: LINDA PERRY

UK PEAK CHART: 1

'Beautiful' is featured on Christina Aguilera's fourth studio album, *Stripped*.

It is a pop ballad written by Linda Perry. The song was awarded a Grammy for Best Female Song Performance. 'Beautiful' has become an anthem for the Gay and Transgender community for its message of self empowerment and inner beauty. The lyrics discuss self esteem and insecurity and Aguilera's vocal performance is powerful and soulful. Elvis Costello covered the song for the TV series House.

Christina Maria Aguilera was born in Staten Island, New York, in 1980. Interested in music from a young age and graced with a powerful voice, Christina had a peripatetic childhood due to her father's army career. Her early success had her pigeonholed in a young pop bracket. She fought to break away from it and the managerial control this implied. This road eventually led to the release of *Stripped* in 2002. The record received critical acclaim and was commercially successful, selling 12 million copies worldwide.

Aguilera has explored different styles such as jazz, blues and soul in further records. Etta James, Whitney Houston and Mariah Carey are acknowledged by her as influential to her vocal approach. She also blends elements of R&B and electronic music with her brand of pop. Her voice is powerful and distinctive and has

inspired the likes of Demi Lovato, Kelly Clarkson and Lady Gaga.

Beautiful

Christina Aguilera

Arranged by Carl Orr

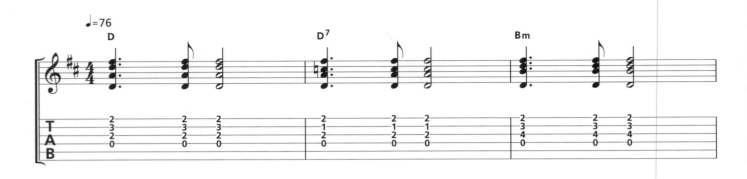

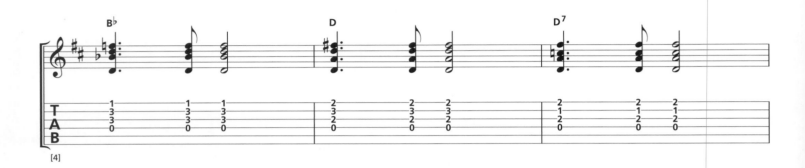

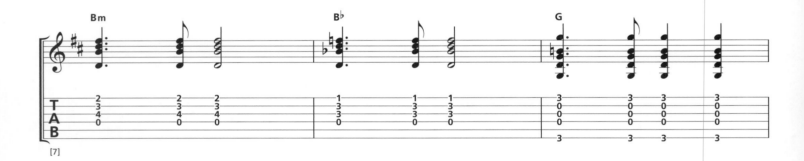

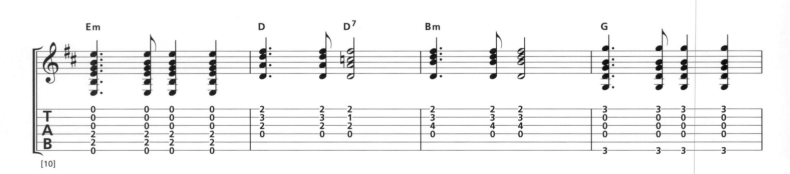

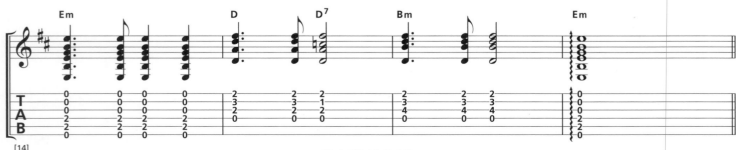

Beautiful | Technical Guidance

This arrangement of Christina Aguilera's haunting song 'Beautiful' features both chords and melody. The first section chords (bars 1–9) are played with a simple, repetitive rhythm. In the second section, starting at bar 10, the rhythm changes slightly, but it is still very simple and steady.

It is very important to play the chords cleanly, with each note ringing clearly with no buzzing or dead notes.

It is advisable to practise each individual change of chords repeatedly. Starting with the first two chords: D to D^7. Then from D^7 to B minor and so on. Applying this exercise to every chord transition will help make them smoother. When each passage can be played smoothly, they can be joined together and played as a whole section (bars 1 to 17).

The vocal melody (bars 18–35) is quite easy. It's all within the first five frets of the top three strings. There are a few interesting notes. The B♭ that occurs in bars 21 and 25 gives the melody a melancholy quality, especially when heard against the accompanying B♭ major chord. It's important to play the melody confidently. As with the chords, it's advisable to break it down into smaller components; for example bars 18–21 comprise a phrase, as do bars 22–25. Each phrase should be practised separately until it can be executed confidently, then the phrases can be put together, eventually playing the whole melody from bar 18 to the end.

You may be able to improve on the lyricism and delivery of the melody by imagining that you are singing the melodic line, telling a story as you play.

This song presents the student with some interesting challenges. It's an attractive song with a lot of emotional impact.

Ray Charles | Stella By Starlight

SONG TITLE: STELLA BY STARLIGHT
ALBUM: DEDICATED TO YOU
LABEL: ABC / PARAMOUNT
GENRE: SOUL
WRITTEN BY: VICTOR YOUNG
PRODUCER: RAY CHARLES

'Stella By Starlight' was written by Victor Young and is one of the most popular jazz standards. The lyrics were written by Ned Washington. The song was recorded first by Charlie Parker, followed by Frank Sinatra, Stan Getz, Bud Powell, Nat King Cole, Larry Coryell and Ray Charles amongst many others.

Ray Charles' version is featured in the film *Casino*. The original cut of the song, from 1944, was featured in the film *The Uninvited*.

Ray Charles Robinson (Ray Charles) was born in Albany, Georgia, in 1930. He died in 2004 in Beverly Hills, California.

Ray Charles was blind from the age of seven. He cites Nat King Cole as a significant influence but his music was also influenced by jazz, blues, rhythm and blues and country music.

Ray Charles pioneered the soul music genre and was the first African-American musician granted artistic control by a mainstream record company.

He had a strong friendship with Quincy Jones, who showed him the ropes of the music business. Ray Charles was regarded as a genius by many, including Frank Sinatra, but he downplayed this notion. He was a consummate pianist and arranger and was one of

the most recognisable voices in American music. He is acknowledged as an influence by Van Morrison, Stevie Wonder, Elvis Presley and Aretha Franklin, amongst many others.

By the mid 60s he was an established star, blending genres and pushing boundaries. His versions of 'What'd I Say' and 'Georgia On My Mind' are now regarded as classics. Although his commercial success diminished with the advent of rock, his music regained popularity in the mid 80s. He was awarded 12 Grammys.

Stella By Starlight

Ray Charles

Arranged by Andy G Jones

♩=145

See note on welcome page about assessed and non-assessed guitar parts

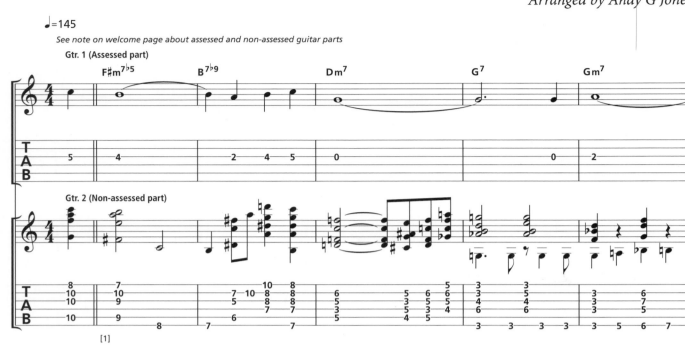

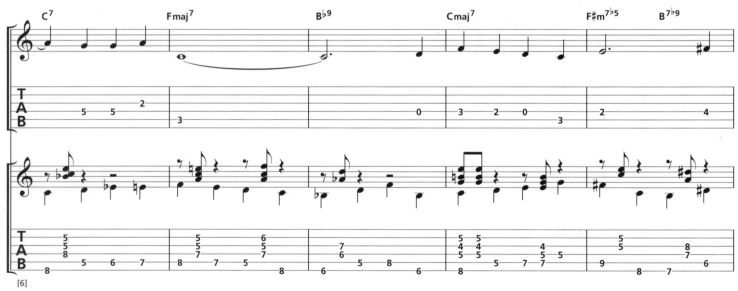

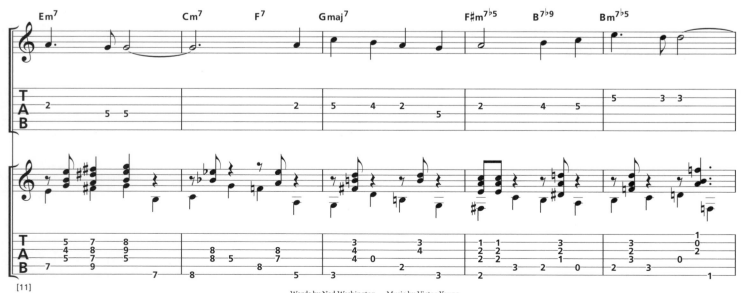

Acoustic Guitar Grade 1

16

Words by Ned Washington   Music by Victor Young
© Copyright 1944 Catherine Hinen/Sony/ATV Harmony
Shapiro Bernstein & Company Limited/Famous Music Corporation.
All Rights Reserved. International Copyright Secured.

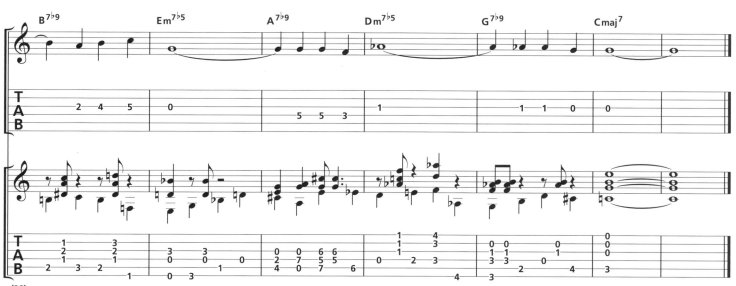

Stella By Starlight | Technical Guidance

The chord changes of 'Stella By Starlight' cover a lot of harmonic ground. This may be one reason for its popularity amongst jazz musicians. It is an interesting framework for improvisation.

This arrangement features the melody. As always with jazz tunes, it is a great basis for improvisation.

In this melody many notes are of interest in terms of their relation to the harmony. For instance, bar 2 features the flattened 9th as the last note. This is a bold note to use over this chord – as a result you'll see that the chord symbol has been adjusted to suggest that this note should be played to accommodate the melody. In bar 5, the melody holds the 9th degree over a minor chord – this is a lovely open sound and a piano player would often take account of this note in their improvised accompaniment.

The first note on bar 9 has an interesting flavour. It is the 4th degree of the C major 7th chord (F). Often, a perfect 4th over major harmony would be avoided by improvisers but it's just a passing note and creates a little tension before moving to the 3rd of the chord (E) which sits more comfortably. The same approach is taken in relation to the Gmaj^7 chord in bar 13 to much the same effect. The melody starts on the 4th degree of E minor 7th on bar 11. In minor chords the 4th is a pleasing and open sound. Jazz musicians make a science and an art of choosing tensions to be used over the different chords when improvising. The 4th degree is exploited again over a minor 7th chord in bar 20.

This tune is peppered with syncopated rhythms. Note the triplet rhythm in bar 20. This is where you play three notes in the space of two. Practise this over a metronome tapping out two clicks until you can comfortably place three notes on top. Start by clapping a triplet pulse and when that feels comfortable pick up your guitar and try it on one note.

Also note how bars 25–30 feature a 'cycle' of half diminished and 7th chords. This is a good melody with which to learn the sound of the flattened 5th on the minor 7th flat five chord.

The accompaniment for this tune is another guitar which plays a 'walking bass line' with chords on top to outline the harmony more fully. This would be a common approach in a jazz guitar duo setting.

The Beatles | Let It Be

SONG TITLE: LET IT BE
ALBUM: LET IT BE / 1970
LABEL: APPLE
GENRE: ROCK / POP
WRITTEN BY: PAUL MCCARTNEY
GUITAR: PAUL MCCARTNEY AND
GEORGE HARRISON
PRODUCER: PHIL SPECTOR
UK PEAK CHART: 1

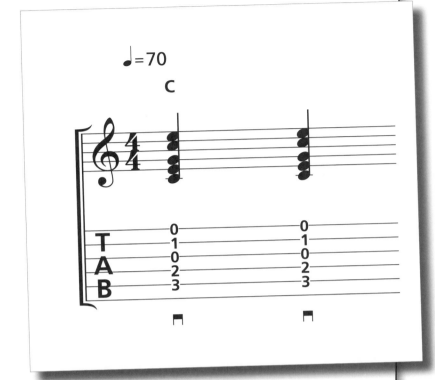

'Let It Be' was written by Paul McCartney in 1968. The lyrics reflect on a dream McCartney had about his mother, Mary, who died when he was fourteen. There is an interplay with biblical references that lead to some confusion about the song's meaning.

'Let It Be' went straight to number one on both sides of the Atlantic. The song is featured on the album of the same title. It was The Beatles' last, after a period of tensions and acrimony. The album's sound was an attempt to recapture some of the early, simpler and rawer sound of the band.

The Beatles are, arguably, the most famous and successful band in history. They have sold around 600 million albums, with estimates reaching one billion.

They have received a plethora of awards and are acknowledged as the creators of a unique stylistic blend that defined pop culture.

The band formed in Liverpool in 1960 and in their 10 year existence they spearheaded a cultural revolution of unparalleled proportions. Their catalogue has been covered by many artists from the world of pop, jazz, rock and classical music.

Let It Be

Arranged by James Betteridge

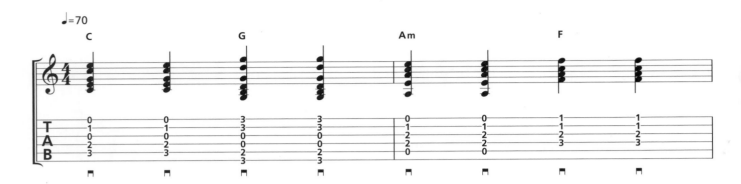

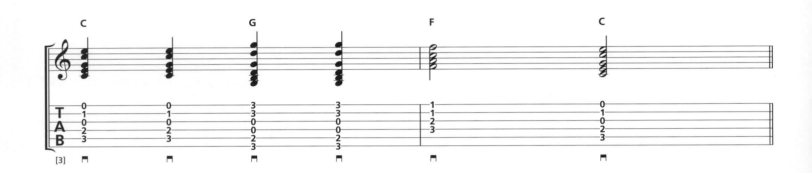

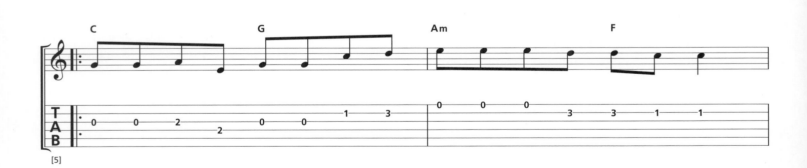

Acoustic Guitar Grade 1

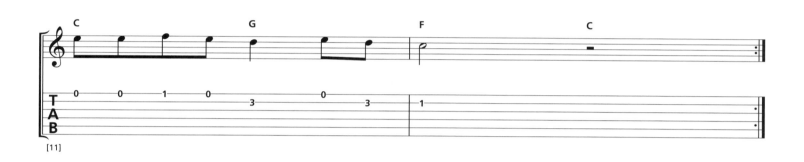

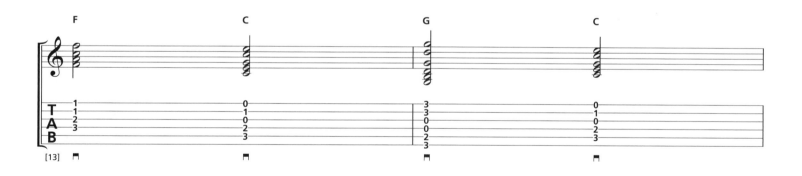

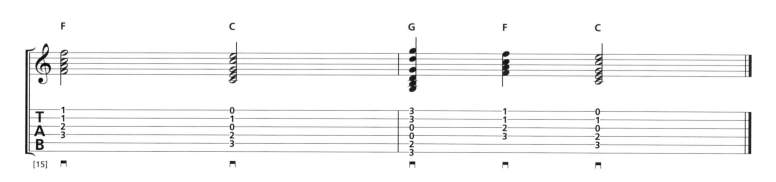

Let It Be | Technical Guidance

'Let It Be' is in the key of C major and uses C major (tonic) , F major (subdominant), G major (dominant) and A minor (submediant). To help illustrate this, the diagram shows the seven diatonic chords of the C major scale.

The C major scale:

I	II	III	IV	V	VI	VII
C maj	Dm	Em	F maj	G maj	Am	B dim
C maj			F maj	G maj	Am	

The same four chords (I, IV, V and VIm) in a variety of keys will provide you with the tools to play thousands of songs across a number of different styles and genres.

This arrangement contains chords and melodic passages. It has been designed to help develop rhythm and single note playing. It is also a good exercise in playing in open position.

It is advisable to split the chords and melody into separate exercises to begin with, making sure the transition between the chord changes is smooth. The F major barre chord will take a little time to get used to. It is important to practise it slowly and making sure all the notes can be heard clearly.

When playing the melody, the main focus should be on picking the notes cleanly without any unwanted strings or string noise being heard. If using a pick, it is advisable to try alternate picking (down and up strokes) to play the melody, trying to make a clean contact with the strings. Once both parts are working, they can be pieced together.

Controlled and minimal movement from the left and right hands can help with technique and sound production.

As with any new piece of music, it is advisable to slow it down first and gradually work up to tempo focusing on accuracy first.

Adele | Someone Like You

SONG TITLE: SOMEONE LIKE YOU
ALBUM: ADELE
LABEL: XL RECORDINGS
GENRE: SOUL, POP
WRITTEN BY: ADELE AND
DAN WILSON
PRODUCER: ADELE AND
DAN WILSON
UK PEAK CHART: 1

'Someone Like You' was written by Adele in collaboration with American songwriter Dan Wilson. The song is featured in Adele's 21 and is an epilogue of sorts to the record's lyrical content, based on the breakup of a two year relationship Adele had with a man, who shortly after their break up married and settled down.

The song was critically acclaimed and had huge international commercial success.

Adele Laurie Blue Adkins was born in London in 1988. She graduated from the BRIT School of Art and Technology in 2006. Soon after she signed to XL Recordings and had a meteoric rise to fame. She released three records to date, 19, 21 and 25. All three were record breaking successes. Adele recorded the title track to the Bond film 'Skyfall'. She co-wrote it with producer Paul Epworth. The song was a worldwide success and was awarded an Oscar. Adele was awarded 10 Grammys and has sold over 50 million records to date.

She is an outspoken celebrity, holding feminist views and defending her looks in an industry obsessed with thin and objectified girls. Her lyrics are personal and heartfelt and her songwriting ability has been praised by the likes of Dave Grohl, Patti Labelle, Celine Dion, Axl Rose, Slash, Stevie Nicks, Pharrell Williams and Madonna, amongst many others. Her influences are wide and include the Spice Girls, Dusty Springfield, Etta James, Ella Fitzgerald, Alabama Shakes and Amy Winehouse.

Someone Like You

Adele

Arranged by Carl Orr

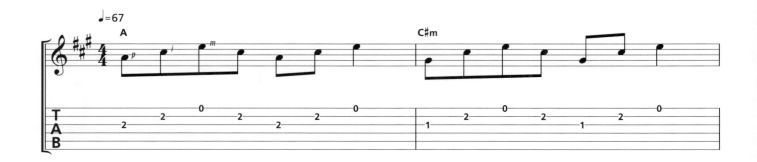

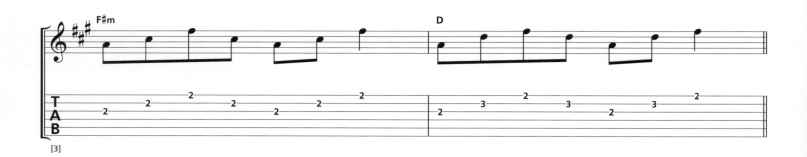

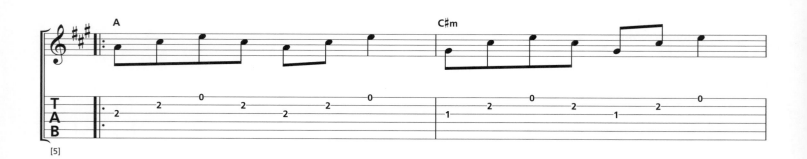

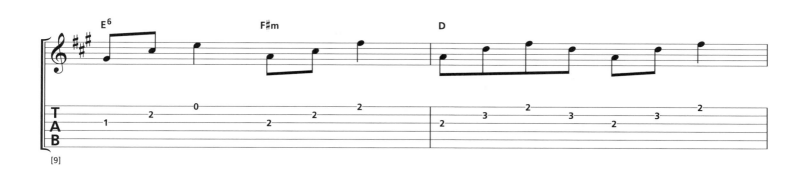

[9]

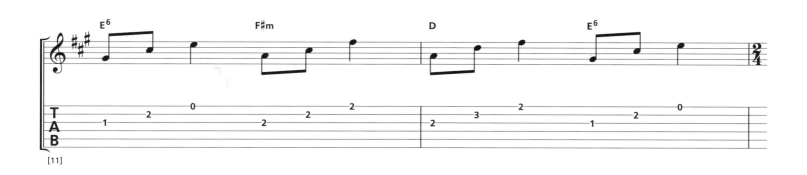

[11]

[13]

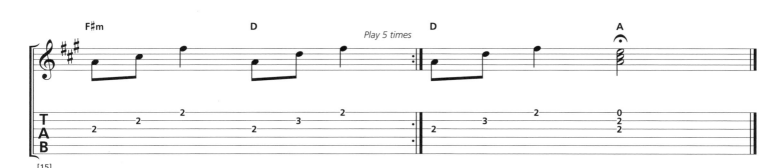

[15]

Someone Like You | Technical Guidance

The verse section is a repeated pattern of A major (I/tonic), C♯minor (III/mediant), F♯minor (VI/submediant) and D major (IV/subdominant), creating a solid and melancholy backdrop to Adele's gospel influenced and freestyling melody. The link section (bars 9–13) comprises three chords, the slightly unusual E^6 (V) chord (the 6th is a less dramatic chord than the dominant but it lends the song a unique character), followed by F♯minor (VI) and D major (IV). These chords are repeated, followed by another E^6 chord and a 2/4 bar of D major (IV). The 2/4 bar (13) creates a slight feeling of surprise and anticipation as the chord needs to resolve. The chorus section (bar 14–15 / repeated five times) starts with an A major chord (tonic), resolving the D major chord from the link section, followed by E major (V), F♯minor and D major, with only half a bar on each chord, so the chords are moving twice as fast as the chords in the verse section, creating a feeling of urgency and momentum. Again, at the end of the song (bar 16), the D major (IV) chord holds on for longer than expected, creating tension until it resolves to the tonic in the second half of the bar.

For this arrangement of Adele's heartbreaking 'Someone Like You', the famous piano part is emulated by the guitar. As in the original, the chords are played in arpeggios from start to finish. It is advisable to play with thumb and fingers, rather than a plectrum. A basic classical guitar style will assign the thumb to the G string, the first finger to the B string and the second finger to the high E string. This way, the picking hand does not need to move around. There are, however, no indications of left hand fingering so teacher and pupil can figure out what works best.

It's important to play consistently throughout, making each note approximately the same in volume. The song is very pianistic, so it has been arranged in a way that sits more naturally on the guitar. With a little work it will feel smooth and will flow well. Imagining it is played on a piano with the sustain pedal down, with each note running into the next whenever possible, will create a good legato feel.

Tom Petty | Free Fallin'

SONG TITLE: FREE FALLIN'

ALBUM: FULL MOON FEVER

LABEL: MCA RECORDS

GENRE: HEARTLAND / ADULT ROCK

WRITTEN BY: TOM PETTY AND
JEFF LYNNE

GUITAR: TOM PETTY AND
MIKE CAMPBELL

PRODUCER: JEFF LYNNE,
TOM PETTY AND
MIKE CAMPBELL

UK PEAK CHART: 59

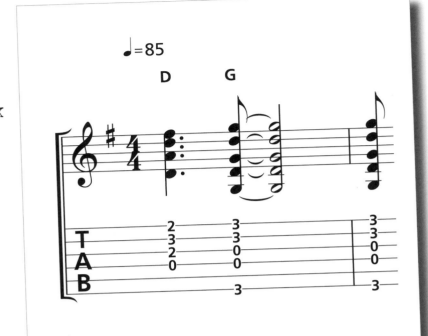

'Free Fallin' is featured in Tom Petty's 1988 solo debut, *Full Moon Fever*. It was co-written by Tom Petty and Jeff Lynne (from ELO fame) who played bass and sang backing vocals on the recording. The song's lyrics are about nostalgia and the feelings for the childhood sweetheart Petty left behind in search of success.

The song has been covered by many artists since its release. These include De La Soul, Stevie Nicks, Tony Hadley and Keith Urban amongst many others. John Mayer covered the song in 2008 to great critical acclaim. 'Free Fallin' is featured in the video game *Lego Rock Band*.

Tom Petty was born in 1950 and is best known for his work with Tom Petty and the Heartbreakers. The band enjoyed much success in the late 70's and early 80's. He also co-founded The Traveling Wilburys with Jeff Lynne and George Harrison. His brand of rootsy, American rock and roll finds resonance across generations and he plays to sold out audiences. Petty has sold over 80 million records. He was inducted into the Rock and Roll Hall of Fame in 2002.

Petty is an outspoken musician with staunch views on artistic control. He had legal disputes with his label ABC Records over transfer to MCA Records and over the pricing of his releases.

Free Fallin'

Tom Petty

Arranged by Andy G Jones

Acoustic Guitar Grade 1

28

Words & Music by Tom Petty & Jeff Lynne

Free Fallin' | Technical Guidance

As with Van Morrison, it's often surprising how interesting Petty's tunes can be despite a relatively small harmonic 'palette'. The use of the A sus^4 voicings adds interest to this progression. Many songwriters would have simply made this an A chord. There are also many subtle voicings that might be attributed to Jeff Lynne, who co-wrote the song and whose harmonic sophistication was brought to bear on this tune. These elements are unexpected and breathe life into a song.

The rhythms of the song are quite syncopated, with many notes anticipating the beat. This is another device that adds musical interest. The melody starts with an anacrusis on the last semiquavers of bar 4. The second note on bar 5 (D) lands on the upbeat of beat 2.

It is advisable to see rhythms related to a grid of subdivisions. In this case mostly quavers (8th notes). Writing where the notes fall above the stave might help relating it to the 1+2+3+4+ subdivision of the bar into quavers. This can be further subdivided into semiquavers (16th notes). Although this approach might seem mathematical, this process is a useful stage before playing music.

The range of notes played in this piece is relatively small. As your musicianship develops you will learn where and how to add some degree of embellishment to the melodies you play.

One way of achieving variation is to consider where to place the picking hand on the string. Picking closer to the bridge sounds sharper, whereas picking further away from it sounds progressively warmer.

This piece could just as easily be played with a pick or fingerstyle.

Technical Exercises

In this section, you will be asked to play a selection of exercises, chosen by the examiner, from each of the groups below.

All exercises need to be played in straight feel, in the keys, octaves and tempos shown. You may use your book for Group A and Group B. All Group C exercises must be played from memory.

Note that Groups A and B need to be played to a click and any fingerings shown are suggestions only.

Group A: Scales
The tempo for this group is ♩=60 bpm.

1. F major scale | Ascending first

2. F major scale | Descending first

3. G major scale | Ascending first

4. G major scale | Descending first

5. D natural minor scale | Ascending first

6. D natural minor scale | Descending first

7. E natural minor scale | Ascending first

8. E natural minor scale | Descending first

9. C dorian mode | Ascending first

10. C dorian mode | Descending first

11. C harmonic minor scale | Ascending first

12. C harmonic minor scale | Descending first

Group B: Broken Chords
The tempo for this group is ♩=100 bpm.

1. F major broken chord

2. F major broken chord

3. G major broken chord

4. G major broken chord

5. D minor broken chord

6. D minor broken chord

7. E minor broken chord

8. E minor broken chord

9. C augmented broken chord

10. C augmented broken chord

11. C diminished broken chord

12. C diminished broken chord

Group C: Chord Voicings

In the exam you will be asked to play, from memory, your choice of one chord voicing from each of the following exercises, without the aid of a backing track or metronome. However, for practice purposes a demonstration of the chords played to a metronome click is available in the downloadable audio.

1. C diminished

2. C augmented

Sight Reading

In this section you have a choice between either a sight reading test or an improvisation and interpretation test (see facing page).

The examiner will ask you which one you wish to choose before commencing. Once you have decided you cannot change your mind.

In the sight reading test, the examiner will give you a 4–6 bar melody in the key of F major or G major. You will first be given 90 seconds to practise, after which the examiner will play the backing track twice. The first time is for you to practise and the second time is for you to perform the final version for the exam. For each playthrough, the backing track will begin with a one bar count-in. The tempo is ♩ = 70.

During the practice time, you will be given the choice of a metronome click throughout or a one bar count-in at the beginning.

The backing track is continuous, so once the first playthrough has finished, the count-in of the second playing will start immediately.

Sight Reading | Example 1

Please note: The test shown is an example. The examiner will give you a different version in the exam.

Sight Reading | Example 2

Please note: The test shown is an example. The examiner will give you a different version in the exam.

Improvisation & Interpretation

In the improvisation and interpretation test, the examiner will give you a 4–6 bar chord progression in the key of F major or G major. You will first be given 90 seconds to practise, after which the examiner will play the backing track twice. The first time is for you to practise and the second time is for you to perform the final version for the exam. For each playthrough, the backing track will begin with a one bar count-in. The tempo is ♩ = 70.

During the practice time, you will be given the choice of a metronome click throughout or a one bar count-in at the beginning.

The backing track is continuous, so once the first playthrough has finished, the count-in of the second playing will start immediately.

You are only required to improvise single note melodies.

Improvisation & Interpretation | Example 1

Please note: The test shown is an example. The examiner will give you a different version in the exam.

Improvisation & Interpretation | Example 2

Please note: The test shown is an example. The examiner will give you a different version in the exam.

Ear Tests

In this section, there are two ear tests:
- Melodic Recall
- Chord Recognition

You will find one example of each type of test printed below and you will need to perform both of them in the exam.

Test 1: Melodic Recall

The examiner will play you three consecutive notes. You will need to identify whether the last two notes are higher or lower in sequence. This means you will need to tell the examiner whether the second note is higher or lower than the first, and whether the third note is higher or lower than the second. You will hear the test twice, each time with a one bar count-in. The tempo is ♩=95 bpm.

For this exercise, please use the words 'higher' and 'lower' in your answer.

Please note: The test shown is an example. The examiner will give you a different version in the exam.

Test 2: Chord Recognition

The examiner will play you a sequence of chords, each with a C root note. You will hear the chord sequence twice, each time with a one bar count-in. You will then be asked to identify the chord quality of each chord, from a choice of major, minor, diminished and augmented. The tempo is ♩=95 bpm.

Please note: The test shown is an example. The examiner will give you a different version in the exam.

General Musicianship Questions

The final part of your exam is the General Musicianship Questions section, which features 5 questions relating to one of your choice of the performance pieces.

1. You will be asked a question relating to the harmony from a section of one of your pieces.

2. You will be asked a question relating to the melody in a section of one of your pieces.

3. You will be asked a question relating to the rhythms used in a section of one of your pieces.

4. You will be asked a question relating to the technical requirements of one of your pieces.

5. You will be asked a question relating to the genre of one of your pieces.

Entering Rockschool Exams

Entering a Rockschool exam is easy, just go online and follow our simple six step process. All details for entering online, dates, fees, regulations and Free Choice pieces can be found at *www.rslawards.com*

- All candidates should ensure they bring their own Grade syllabus book to the exam or have proof of digital purchase ready to show the examiner.

- All Grade 6–8 candidates must ensure that they bring valid photo ID to their exam.

Marking Schemes

ELEMENT	PASS	MERIT	DISTINCTION
Performance Piece 1	12–14 out of 20	15–17 out of 20	18+ out of 20
Performance Piece 2	12–14 out of 20	15–17 out of 20	18+ out of 20
Performance Piece 3	12–14 out of 20	15–17 out of 20	18+ out of 20
Technical Exercises	9–10 out of 15	11–12 out of 15	13+ out of 15
Sight Reading *or* Improvisation & Interpretation	6 out of 10	7–8 out of 10	9+ out of 10
Ear Tests	6 out of 10	7–8 out of 10	9+ out of 10
General Musicianship Questions	3 out of 5	4 out of 5	5 out of 5
TOTAL MARKS	60%+	74%+	90%+

GRADE EXAMS | GRADES 6–8

ELEMENT	PASS	MERIT	DISTINCTION
Performance Piece 1	12–14 out of 20	15–17 out of 20	18+ out of 20
Performance Piece 2	12–14 out of 20	15–17 out of 20	18+ out of 20
Performance Piece 3	12–14 out of 20	15–17 out of 20	18+ out of 20
Technical Exercises	9–10 out of 15	11–12 out of 15	13+ out of 15
Quick Study Piece	6 out of 10	7–8 out of 10	9+ out of 10
Ear Tests	6 out of 10	7–8 out of 10	9+ out of 10
General Musicianship Questions	3 out of 5	4 out of 5	5 out of 5
TOTAL MARKS	60%+	74%+	90%+

PERFORMANCE CERTIFICATES | DEBUT TO GRADE 8 *

ELEMENT	PASS	MERIT	DISTINCTION
Performance Piece 1	12–14 out of 20	15–17 out of 20	18+ out of 20
Performance Piece 2	12–14 out of 20	15–17 out of 20	18+ out of 20
Performance Piece 3	12–14 out of 20	15–17 out of 20	18+ out of 20
Performance Piece 4	12–14 out of 20	15–17 out of 20	18+ out of 20
Performance Piece 5	12–14 out of 20	15–17 out of 20	18+ out of 20
TOTAL MARKS	60%+	75%+	90%+

* Note that there are no Debut Vocal exams.

Copyright Information

Let It Be
(Lennon/McCartney)
Sony/ATV Music Publishing (UK) Limited

The Unforgiven
(Hetfield/Hammett/Ulrich)
Universal Music Publishing Limited

Someone Like You
(Adkins/Wilson)
Chrysalis-Music-Ltd/Universal Music Publishing Limited

Free Fallin'
(Petty/Lynne)
Wixen Music UK Ltd/EMI Music Publishing Ltd

Beautiful
(Perry)
Sony/ATV Harmony UK

Stella By Starlight
(Washington/Young)
Shapiro Bernstein & Co Limited/Sony/ATV Harmony UK

mcps

rockschool®

DIGITAL DOWNLOADS NOW AVAILABLE!

All your favourite Rockschool titles are now available to download instantly from the RSL shop. Download entire grade books, individual tracks or supporting tests to all your devices.

START DOWNLOADING NOW

www.rslawards.com/shop